GENGHIS SWAN

A juicy, true story about a naughty swan

in Plymouth, MA

GENGHIS SWAN

A juicy, true story about a naughty swan

in Plymouth, MA

Written by Deanna Penkus Nealey

Illustrated by Lauren Buckman Jezierski

Riverhaven Books

www.RiverhavenBooks.com

Published in the United States by Riverhaven Books
www.RiverhavenBooks.com

ISBN: 978-1-937588-34-2

Printed in the United States of America
by Country Press, Lakeville, Massachusetts

This book is dedicated to all of the children who will read it or hear this story.

For my children,
Tara, Krista, Rebecca, and Justin,
and my grandchildren,
Cassie, Braham, Ellise, Maylen, Justin and Krista,
with
special thanks to
Judith Campbell for her support
and
Lauren Buckman Jezierski
for bringing this story
to life
through her beautiful artwork

This story is about caring adults teaching a naughty swan that he has choices and consequences for his actions. It is a success story of a creative plan to change the bad behavior of a young swan. Genghis Swan is a lovable character, who I hope still lives on the Eel River now as a responsible parent himself

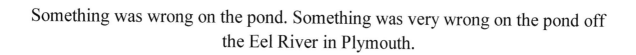

Something was wrong on the pond. Something was very wrong on the pond off the Eel River in Plymouth.

It all started when a new young swan arrived on the river and quickly disturbed the peace of the other beautiful white swans that lived there, called "mute swans."

The new swan was a bully.
He did not want to share the river with anyone else.

He hissed
     and he snorted
          and he flapped his wings
               to scare people away from enjoying the water on boats or canoes.

Once he even tipped over a boat full of people!

The local newspaper wrote a story about him and held a contest to give him a name.

"Genghis Swan" was picked because it was the name of a cruel king named Genghis Khan, who lived in China many years ago.

The town held a meeting to ask people what to do about Genghis Swan.
They even put up a sign that said—BEWARE OF THE SWAN.

Angry people wanted to move Genghis far away.
They all just wanted to get rid of the bad swan.

But there was a big problem.

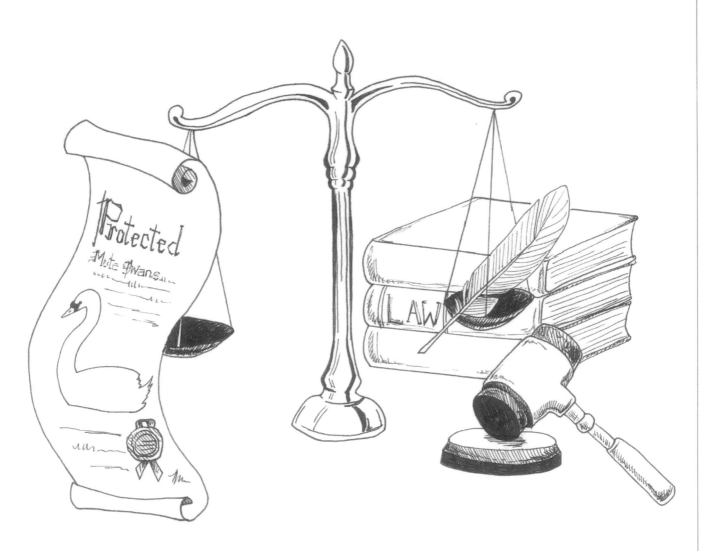

There is a law that says swans and other wild animals cannot be
hurt or moved from their homes.

How could they let Genghis stay on the river?
How could he learn to share the river and not
be a bully anymore?

Some people who loved animals and wanted to protect them had an
idea. It would not hurt Genghis, but it should teach him to share the
river with others. It was like sending him to obedience school!

Every time Genghis came near their boat, they would squirt grape juice at him.

It could not be apple juice or orange juice. It had to
be grape juice, because swans hate grape juice!

So, every time Genghis came close to their boat, he got a snootful of grape juice from a super soaker! He hated the taste and his white feathers were turning purple!

Genghis had to make a choice to either stop bullying people or to get squirted with grape juice.
He definitely did not want to turn into a purple swan!

After several times, he finally made the right
choice to share the river with others, and he
learned not to be a troublemaker anymore.

Everyone was glad that this juicy plan had worked for Genghis. Squirting grape juice worked for a naughty swan, but it never would work for naughty children!

The people of Plymouth were happy that they had given Genghis a chance to learn how to
become a better swan. So they wanted to give him a special reward.
They decided to take down the sign that said BEWARE OF THE SWAN
because it was no longer needed.

Genghis had changed his bad behavior and proved that he was not a danger anymore to people on the river. He was a very proud graduate of "obedience school" for swans.

Now something was good. Something was very good on the pond off the Eel River.

Genghis Swan could stay at home, where he belonged.

To learn more about the true story, please visit "The Education of Ghengis Swan"
by Mary Baird, The Humane Society of the US, Sept. 25, 2009
http://www.humanesociety.org/animals/swans/tips/the_education_of_genghis_swan.